Almost Gone

The World's Rarest Animals

MONKEY-EATING EAGLE

The Philippines • Fewer than 300 left

This fierce hunter is the national bird of the Philippines. The monkey-eating eagle is large, standing three feet tall with a six-and-a-half-foot wingspan and a long, sharp beak. It lives in tropical rain forests and eats monkeys, squirrels and other small mammals. Like many other endangered animals of the rain forest, it is threatened by the destruction of its habitat. These birds are killed by farmers who mistakenly believe that they feed on their livestock.

STAGE 2

Almost Gone

The World's Rarest Animals

By Steve Jenkins

HarperCollins*Publishers*

For Page, Alec and Jamie

The *Let's-Read-and-Find-Out Science* book series was originated by Dr. Franklyn M. Branley, Astronomer Emeritus and former Chairman of the American Museum–Hayden Planetarium, and was formerly co-edited by him and Dr. Roma Gans, Professor Emeritus of Childhood Education, Teachers College, Columbia University. Text and illustrations for each of the books in the series are checked for accuracy by an expert in the relevant field. For more information about Let's-Read-and-Find-Out Science books, write to HarperCollins Children's Books, 1350 Avenue of the Americas, New York, NY 10019, or visit our website at www.letsreadandfindout.com.

Library of Congress Cataloging-in-Publication Data
Jenkins, Steve, date.
    Almost gone : the world's rarest animals / by Steve Jenkins.— 1st ed.
        p.   cm. — (Let's-read-and-find-out science. Stage 2)
    ISBN-10: 0-06-053598-9 — ISBN-10: 0-06-053600-4 (pbk.)
    ISBN-13: 978-0-06-053598-8 — ISBN-13: 978-0-06-053600-8 (pbk.)
    1. Rare animals—Juvenile literature. 2. Endangered species—Juvenile literature. I. Title. II. Series.
QL83.J474 2006   2004030199
591.68—dc22   CIP
                                                                                                  AC

Typography by Elynn Cohen   1 2 3 4 5 6 7 8 9 10   ❖   First Edition

CRESTED SHELDUCK

China • Fewer than 100 left*

The crested shelduck was once found
throughout much of East Asia. It has been
hunted for food and for its beautiful feathers,
until it has become one of the most
endangered birds in the world.

---

*ABOUT THE NUMBER OF ANIMALS LEFT:

Animals in the wild are hard to count accurately. The numbers given for each animal
in this book are the best guesses of the scientists who study them. These numbers don't
include animals living in zoos, just those left in their natural habitats. As people become
concerned and take action, many of these numbers will increase. Others, however,
will go down, since it's too late to help all of these animals recover.

INTRODUCTION

There is a bird perched outside your window, a small bird with a black head, a white throat and a gray body. It is a chickadee. Suppose this bird and all the other chickadees in the world died out—became extinct. Would it matter? Well, you'd never again see a chickadee sitting outside your window or flying or feeding its young or building a nest. You'd never again hear a chickadee chirping. And that would be sad. But there is much more to it than that.

Chickadees eat insects. Without chickadees, there would be more insects. Some of these insects would attack the plants in your garden. Others, such as mosquitoes, carry diseases that might make you sick. Chickadees also eat fruit and berries. Their droppings spread and fertilize the seeds.

Hawks eat chickadees. Without chickadees, the hawks might not have enough to eat and would starve or go someplace else. Hawks also eat rats and mice. Without hawks, there would be more rats and mice.

Each chickadee carries thousands, even millions, of tiny mites, lice and bacteria on its feathers and inside its body. Many of these creatures can live nowhere else. Without chickadees, they would die.

Every living thing is connected to many other living things, often in ways we don't understand or even suspect. And once an animal or a plant is gone, it can never come back. All the living things that interact with it will never be the same. Some of them won't be able to survive themselves.

Chickadees, as it turns out, are not in great danger. But many other animals are. All over the world, people are building roads and cities, turning open land into farms and ranches and polluting the air and water. This has put millions of animals at risk. Some are critically endangered and may soon become extinct. Some can be saved if we act quickly to help them. For others, it is already too late.

Here are a few of these animals—animals that are almost gone.

GRAND CAYMAN BLUE IGUANA

Grand Cayman Island, the Caribbean • Fewer than 25 left

This iguana is found on just one island in the Caribbean.
The blue iguana is three to four feet in length, weighs
fifteen to twenty pounds and can live to be fifty
years old. Its body turns bright turquoise during
mating season. Blue iguanas eat fruit, flowers
and leaves. They have been hunted by
people for food, run over by cars
and had their nests destroyed
by wild dogs.

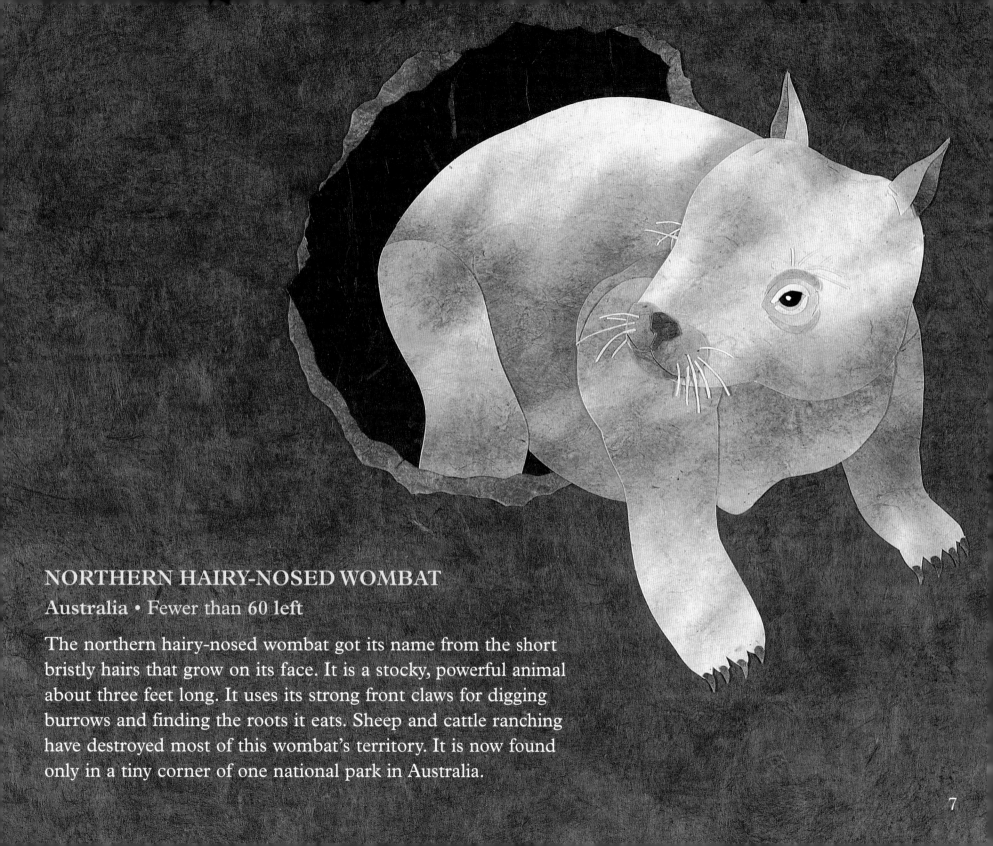

NORTHERN HAIRY-NOSED WOMBAT
Australia • Fewer than 60 left

The northern hairy-nosed wombat got its name from the short bristly hairs that grow on its face. It is a stocky, powerful animal about three feet long. It uses its strong front claws for digging burrows and finding the roots it eats. Sheep and cattle ranching have destroyed most of this wombat's territory. It is now found only in a tiny corner of one national park in Australia.

CALIFORNIA CONDOR

Southwestern United States • Fewer than 200 left

These enormous birds, with a wingspan of more than nine feet, can soar for hours without flapping their wings. Condors are scavengers—they eat dead animals that they spot from the air. By 1982, hunting, loss of habitat, pesticide poisoning and collisions with power lines had left fewer than twenty-five California condors living in the wild. Since then, raising birds in captivity and releasing them into the wild is slowly helping to increase their numbers.

ADDAX

Sahara Desert, Africa • Fewer than 400 left

The addax is a large antelope, weighing up to three hundred pounds. It lives in the hot, dry deserts of northern Africa and may go most of its life without drinking, getting the water it needs from the sparse grasses and bushes it eats. The addax is hunted for its meat and leather, and during the past hundred years its numbers have declined sharply.

9

YANGTZE RIVER DOLPHIN, OR BAIJI
China • Fewer than 20 left

These freshwater dolphins live in small groups along the length of the Yangtze River. They may grow to be eight feet long and weigh up to five hundred pounds. The baiji appear in many Chinese myths and folktales. Pollution, collisions with ships' propellers and construction on the river have greatly endangered these creatures. There were approximately six thousand baiji in the 1950s, a few hundred in the 1980s and fewer than two dozen in 2000.

ASSAM RABBIT, OR HISPID HARE
India and Nepal • Fewer than 110 left

This gentle, slow-moving rabbit is also known as a hispid hare. It is about one and a half feet long and weighs four or five pounds. Assam rabbits live in tall grass in the foothills of the Himalaya Mountains. They eat the roots and young shoots of this grass. The destruction of this habitat to create farmland has made the Assam rabbit extremely rare.

MIAMI BLUE BUTTERFLY

Florida, United States • Fewer than 50 left

For fifty years, no one saw a Miami blue butterfly. Then, in 2000, a colony of these tiny bright blue butterflies was found on an island in the Florida Keys. In many places, development has destroyed this butterfly's habitat and the plants its caterpillars eat. Butterfly collectors and pesticides used to control mosquitoes also threaten the Miami blue butterfly.

JAVAN RHINOCEROS

Vietnam and Indonesia • Fewer than 60 left

Although the Javan rhinoceros once lived throughout Southeast Asia, it is now found in just two national parks in Vietnam and in Indonesia. These rhinos live in dense, low-lying tropical forests, and much of their jungle habitat has been cleared by farming or logging. Their numbers have also been seriously reduced by poaching, or illegal hunting. The hunters are after the rhino's horn, which is in great demand in traditional Asian medicine. Unlike many critically endangered animals, there are no Javan rhinoceroses in captivity.

GOLDEN LION TAMARIN
Brazil • A few hundred left

This squirrel-size monkey lives in the tropical forests on the coast of Brazil. It is omnivorous—it will eat almost anything—including fruit, insects, frogs, lizards and small birds. Golden lion tamarins are preyed upon by eagles, snakes and jaguars, but are endangered mostly because people have destroyed so much of their forest home. A program to breed golden lion tamarins in captivity has increased their numbers in recent years.

EASTERN BARRED BANDICOOT
Australia • Fewer than 300 left

The bandicoot is a marsupial—a mammal that carries its young in a pouch. The eastern barred bandicoot is about the size of a rabbit. It is found in one small part of Australia. A shy, solitary creature, the bandicoot sleeps in burrows during the day and comes out at night to search for grubs, worms, beetles and berries. It uses its excellent sense of smell to find food and its pointed nose and strong claws to dig. The bandicoot is a fast runner and can jump three feet in one leap.

GIANT STICK INSECT
Lord Howe Island, Australia • Fewer than 10 left

A rock rising from the sea near Lord Howe Island is the home of the world's rarest insect, the six-inch-long giant stick insect. It was thought to be extinct since 1918, when a ship ran aground on Lord Howe Island and rats from the ship attacked the giant stick insects living there. A few survived, however, and in 2001, three of the insects were discovered on this rocky outcropping.

DWARF WATER BUFFALO, OR TAMARAW
The Philippines • Fewer than 200 left

At 650 pounds, the dwarf water buffalo, also called the tamaraw, is small for a buffalo. It lives in dense, wet forests on one island in the Philippines, where it feeds on grass and water plants. Much of the forest land where this buffalo lives has been cleared, destroying its food source. Hunting has also helped reduce it numbers.

BACTRIAN CAMEL

Mongolia and China • Fewer than 500 left

Bactrian camels are the two-humped relatives of the more common one-humped camel. They live in the harsh deserts of central Asia. Their humps contain stored fat and allow these camels to go for several days without food or water. Their long, shaggy coats keep them warm in the cold desert nights, and they are able to close their nostrils to keep out blowing sand. In many places, domesticated camels have crowded out their wild Bactrian cousins.

WATERFALL FROG, OR TORRENT FROG

Australia • Unknown number left

The waterfall frog, also called the torrent frog, lives near fast-moving streams and waterfalls in the rain forests of northeastern Australia. Once common, it has almost disappeared in just a few years. No one is sure why this frog and many others around the world have become endangered so quickly. They may be the victims of a new kind of fungus or may be especially sensitive to the effects of global warming.

COELACANTH

Indian Ocean • Unknown number left

Sometimes called "living fossils," these ancient fish
were thought to have disappeared 80 million years ago.
In fact, fossilized coelacanths 360 million years old have
been found. In 1938, a fisherman in the Indian Ocean caught
a coelacanth in his net. Since then, a few more coelacanths
have been caught. The largest was nearly six feet long and
weighed two hundred pounds. Scientists think that these
fish live in caves on the ocean floor.

IRIOMOTE CAT
Japan • Fewer than 100 left

This wild cat lives on only one small Japanese island. It is about two feet long with legs and a tail that are short compared to its body. The Iriomote cat hunts at night and feeds on small mammals, reptiles, birds and fish. It has lost much of its habitat to human activity and faces competition from feral cats—pets that have gone wild.

24

ABINGTON ISLAND TORTOISE
The Galápagos Islands • 1 left

This tortoise, nicknamed "Lonesome George," is the rarest animal in the world. He is probably the last living member of his species. Abington Galápagos tortoises are big enough to ride on—the males can be four feet long and weigh five hundred pounds. The tortoises were overhunted in the 1800s by sailors, who caught them by the thousands and took them on board their ships for food.

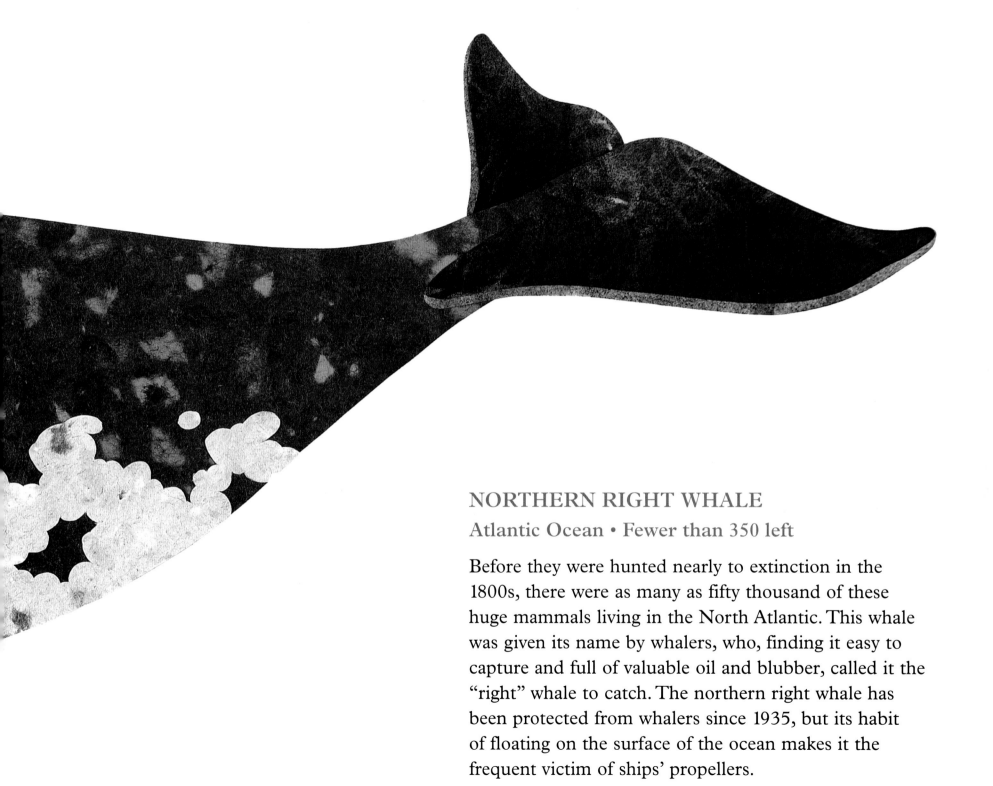

NORTHERN RIGHT WHALE
Atlantic Ocean • Fewer than 350 left

Before they were hunted nearly to extinction in the 1800s, there were as many as fifty thousand of these huge mammals living in the North Atlantic. This whale was given its name by whalers, who, finding it easy to capture and full of valuable oil and blubber, called it the "right" whale to catch. The northern right whale has been protected from whalers since 1935, but its habit of floating on the surface of the ocean makes it the frequent victim of ships' propellers.

GONE FOREVER

These animals are extinct. There is little or no chance that they will be seen again. Because the web of connections among living things is so complex, we don't understand all the consequences of a species becoming extinct. We do know that something unique has been lost and can never be replaced.

MOA
New Zealand • Extinct around 1600

The largest of these flightless birds stood over six feet tall at the shoulder and weighed six hundred pounds. When a big moa held its head high, it measured twelve or thirteen feet tall. For millions of years, these forest dwellers had never seen a human, so they had no natural fear of the first people who arrived on their island home. Within a hundred years of their first encounter with humans, they had been hunted to extinction.

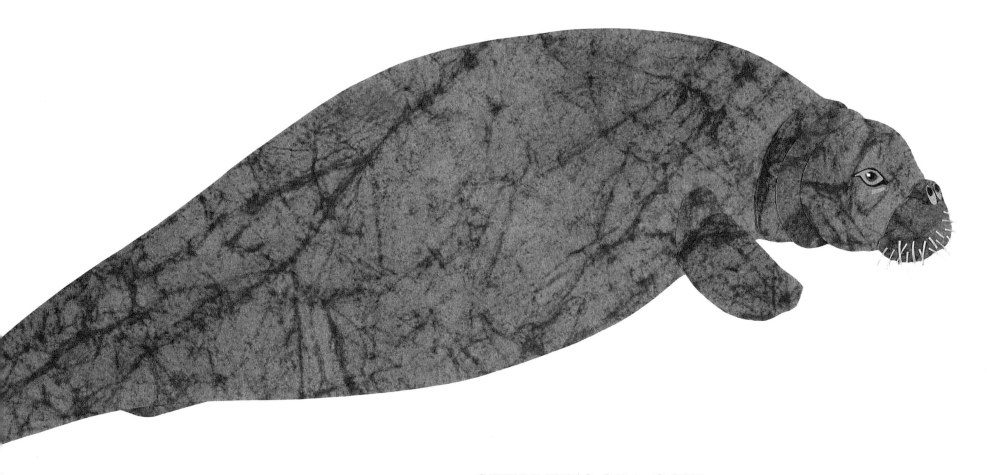

STELLER'S SEA COW
The Bering Strait, between Alaska and Russia
Extinct in 1768

The sea cow was huge—twenty-five feet long and eight thousand pounds. It swam in the cold waters of the northern Pacific. Trappers collecting seal furs hunted the Steller's sea cow for food. The last of the Steller's sea cows died just twenty-seven years after first being described by the naturalist George Steller.

TASMANIAN WOLF, OR THYLACINE

Tasmania, Australia • Last seen in 1936

The Tasmanian wolf, or thylacine, was not really a wolf. It was a marsupial and carried its young in a pouch like a kangaroo. It was named after the island where it was last seen in the wild. It was hunted to extinction by ranchers trying to protect their sheep. For years after the last known Tasmanian wolf died, there were reports of a few animals still living in the wild, but no one has ever found one.

GUAM FLYING FOX
Guam, the Mariana Islands • Last seen in 1974

Little is known about these animals. The Guam flying fox was a kind of bat, named for its pointed face and large ears. It fed at night on flowers and fruit. It is suspected that this bat and many other animals on Guam were killed off by an invasive species: the brown tree snake, which was introduced to their island home in the 1940s. There is little hope that any Guam flying foxes survive today.

COMING BACK

Not all endangered animals necessarily become extinct. Some animals that were almost gone have been able to recover, or at least begin increasing in number. People have acted to protect their habitats, reduce the threat of hunting or collecting and breed animals in captivity to be released back into the wild. It's hard work, but for these animals and all living things on Earth, it has paid off.

GHARIAL, OR INDIAN CROCODILE
Northern India

The gharial, also known as the Indian crocodile, can measure up to twenty feet long, making it one of the largest crocodiles. The gharial's long, thin snout is filled with sharp teeth used for catching fish. Some people believe that the nose of this crocodile has medicinal properties. It has been protected from hunters since the 1970s, when there were only about a hundred left. Today there are several thousand gharials living in the wild.

WHOOPING CRANE
North America

The whooping crane is the largest North American bird. It stands nearly five feet tall, with wings that can measure eight feet from tip to tip. Whooping cranes are migratory birds—they travel each fall from their nesting grounds in central Canada to their wintering grounds on the Gulf Coast of the United States and then back to Canada each spring. This is a long, dangerous journey. By the 1940s, there were only twenty-two whooping cranes left in the world. Breeding and protection programs have increased that number to more than three hundred today.

ALPINE IBEX
Europe

Once common throughout the mountains of central Europe, there were probably fewer than fifty of these mountain goats left in 1900. Alpine ibex were killed for their horns or in the belief that parts of their bodies could cure certain diseases. In the 1950s, several zoos began breeding the Alpine ibex and returning them to the wild. Today there are more than ten thousand Alpine ibex in France, Switzerland, Italy and other European countries.

33

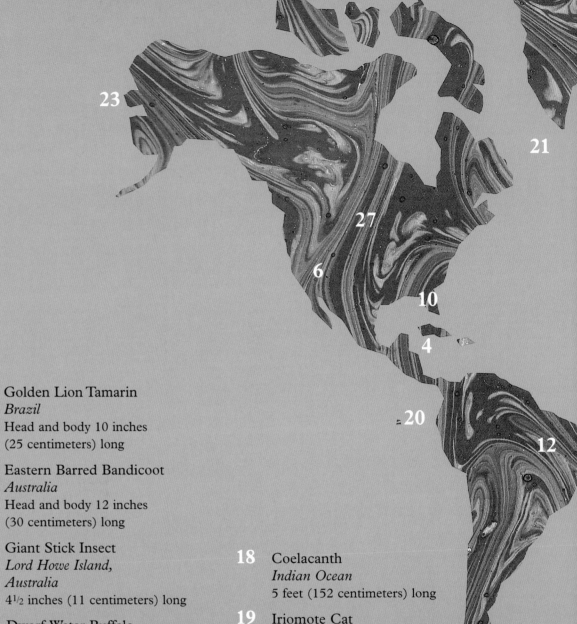

ALMOST GONE

1   Amur Leopard
Siberia (Russia), China and Korea
8 feet (244 centimeters) long, including tail

2   Monkey-Eating Eagle
The Philippines
6½-foot (198-centimeter) wingspan

3   Crested Shelduck
China
25 inches (64 centimeters) long

4   Grand Cayman Blue Iguana
Grand Cayman Island
4 feet (122 centimeters) long, including tail

5   Northern Hairy-Nosed Wombat
Australia
39 inches (99 centimeters) long

6   California Condor
Southwestern United States
9½-foot (290-centimeter) wingspan

7   Addax
Sahara Desert, Africa
63 inches (160 centimeters) long

8   Yangtze River Dolphin
China
8 feet (244 centimeters) long

9   Assam Rabbit
India and Nepal
18 inches (46 centimeters) long

10   Miami Blue Butterfly
Florida, United States
⅝-inch (16-millimeter) wingspan

11   Javan Rhinoceros
Vietnam and Indonesia
10 feet (3 meters) long

12   Golden Lion Tamarin
Brazil
Head and body 10 inches
(25 centimeters) long

13   Eastern Barred Bandicoot
Australia
Head and body 12 inches
(30 centimeters) long

14   Giant Stick Insect
*Lord Howe Island,
Australia*
4½ inches (11 centimeters) long

15   Dwarf Water Buffalo
The Philippines
6 feet (183 centimeters) long

16   Bactrian Camel
Mongolia and China
7 feet (2 meters) tall

17   Waterfall Frog
Australia
2 inches (51 millimeters) long

18   Coelacanth
Indian Ocean
5 feet (152 centimeters) long

19   Iriomote Cat
Japan
20 inches (51 centimeters) long

20   Abington Island Tortoise
The Galápagos Islands
4 feet (122 centimeters) long

21   Northern Right Whale
Atlantic Ocean
50 feet (15 meters) long

25 Guam Flying Fox
Guam
27-inch (69-centimeter) wingspan

GONE FOREVER

22 Moa
New Zealand
6½ feet (198 centimeters)
tall at the shoulder

23 Steller's Sea Cow
The Bering Strait
24 feet (7 meters) long

24 Tasmanian Wolf
Tasmania, Australia
5 feet (152 centimeters) long,
including tail

COMING BACK

26 Gharial
Northern India
20 feet (6 meters) long

27 Whooping Crane
North America
8-foot (244-centimeter) wingspan

28 Alpine Ibex
Europe
5 feet (152 centimeters) long

A note about sizes: Like
people, animals vary in
size. These are the average
sizes of adult animals;
individuals may be larger
or smaller.